COLOR PALETTES

FOR ARTISTS, GRAPHIC DESIGNERS, INTERIOR DESIGNERS & COLORING ENTHUSIASTS

64 INSPIRATIONAL COMBINATIONS WITH
HEX CODES TO SPARK CREATIVITY

VOL. 1

INSTRUCTIONS

Why should I use a color palette?

Using a color palette can help you to create a certain look or mood. Whether it's something fun and vibrant or dark and emotional, it can serve as a great source of inspiration to help you break through creative blocks and give you a starting point when you're stuck for ideas or not sure where to begin.

Browsing color palettes can become a really fun part of your process and exploring new color combinations can be exciting and rewarding. It can help you think of new and unique ways to look at something, like using different colors that you wouldn't normally consider using.

And above all else, it can give you confidence in choosing your colors because you can see how they work together before you begin.

How should I use the color palettes?

Color palettes can be used for so many creative projects. Whether you're an artist, a graphic designer, an interior designer - you can use the color palettes in this book to draw inspiration.

| #9C9FB5 | #526A7D | #90896D | #9D6C69 | #776B2C | #E58990 |

How should I use the color palettes? (cont.)

You can choose as many or as few colors as you like. You can choose to go lighter or darker to expand the range of colors or add highlights and shadows. Or you can simply use them as a starting point and add your own colors.

Each color is printed to the edge of the paper. This is to make color matching easier. Hold the color against your own media to check the similarity. But don't worry if you don't have a perfect match. This is not an exact science and the colors don't have to match exactly to have a good result.

There is a helpful index at the back of this book. If you have a specific color in mind, have a look for it in the index and then look for the corresponding palettes.

HEX Codes

Each color has a corresponding HEX code so that you can recreate the color digitally if you need to. Please note that there may be a slight difference between how colors appear on screen and how they appear in print. It's best to adjust the color by eye if you need to.

All the images in this book are either royalty free stock images, the author's own photographs, or generated by artificial intelligence. This means they are all copyright free, so you are welcome to use the images themselves in any way you wish.

#4F4D25

#262615

#73722C

#D4C8A4

#B6AD3D

#FBB72F

1

2

#F6821E

#CE8EA8

#A6AF94

#315020

#4B6250

#17281A

#25352D

#4B6F6B

#B8BA37

#5A6624

#B2C3A1

#A6B261

3

4

#5A553C

#C2A92A

#252018

#915A38

#BEBCAD

#857D21

#C1C1BD

#858146

#8DC0E3

#7E7D6E

#839427

#1D2F36

5

#EAC7F5

#F64227

#253338

#A8CAD4

#50883D

#789AA5

7

#335250

#6CAFA4

#5AA1D0

#919440

#B36593

#F4D237

8

#69A1A1

#AE8E3D

#DBB037

#645D3D

#5B7379

#283234

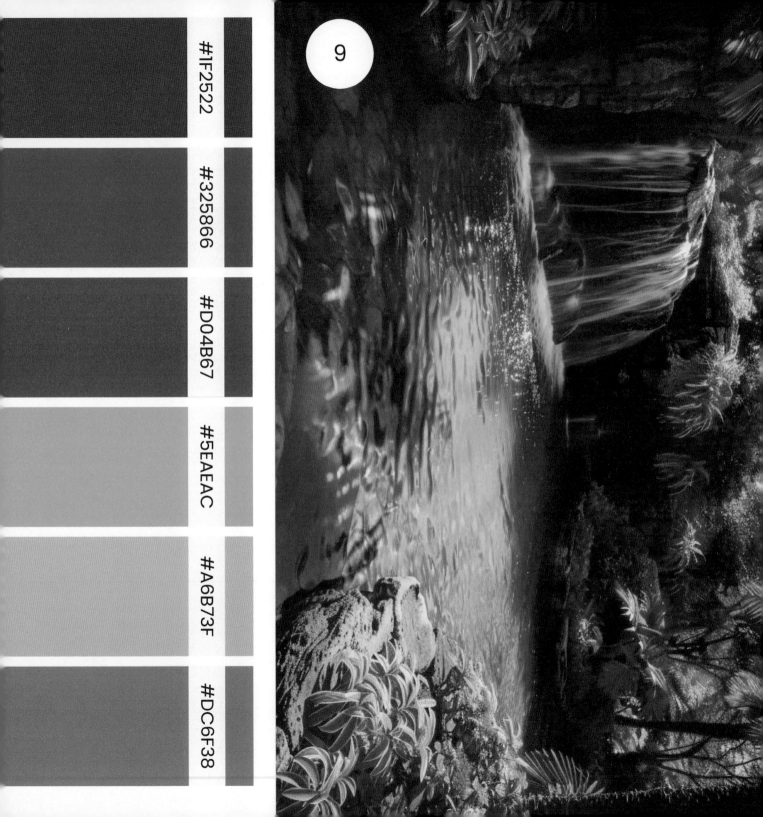

#1F2522

#325866

#D04B67

#5EAEAC

#A6B73F

#DC6F38

9

#A5A89B

#3E332D

#8E653F

#8FA9AE

#BB8242

#568EA9

#7FCED5

#C5DBD6

#469BAC

#928E49

#A07D7F

#C68C21

11

#C8CECD

#706C51

#262F2C

#3F6E70

#B5CAC9

#73A6A7

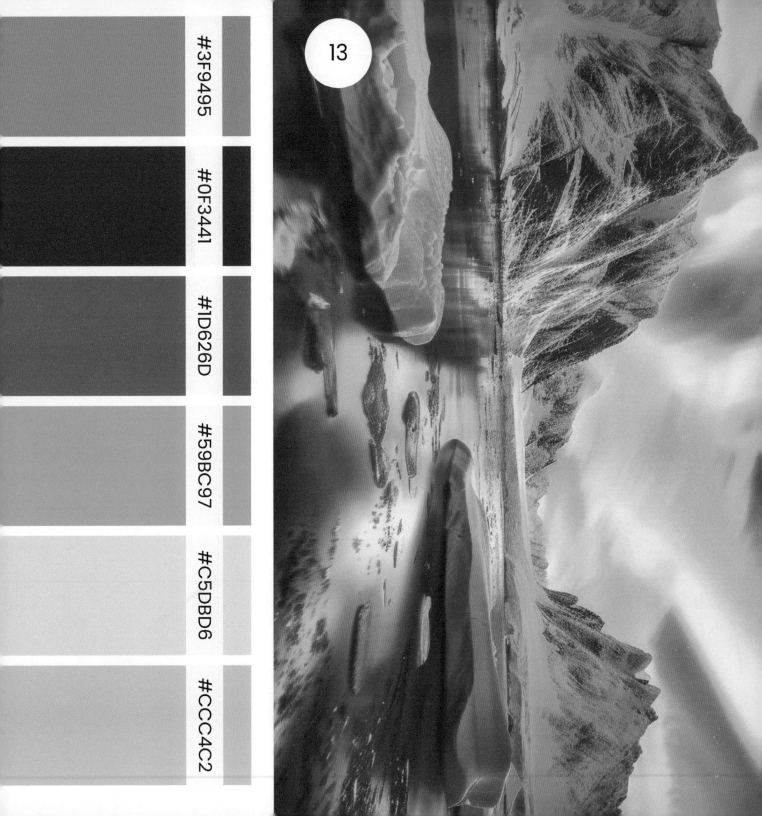

#3F9495

#0F3441

#1D626D

#59BC97

#C5DBD6

#CCC4C2

13

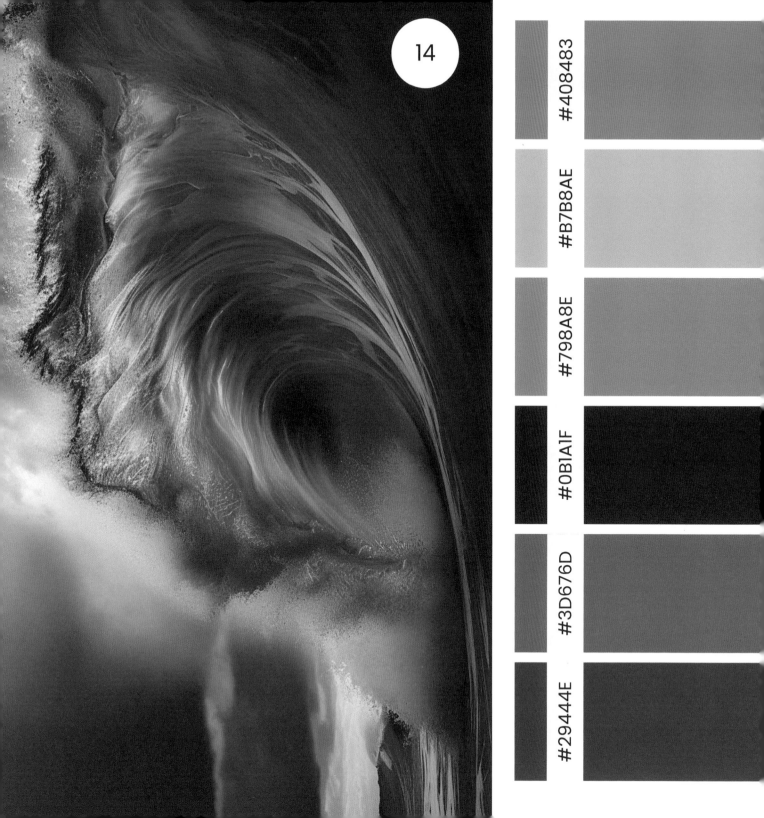

14

#408483

#B7B8AE

#798A8E

#0B1A1F

#3D676D

#29444E

15

#4C7E89

#2A5E6B

#89CFCD

#163F52

#B0C2BD

#F2EACB

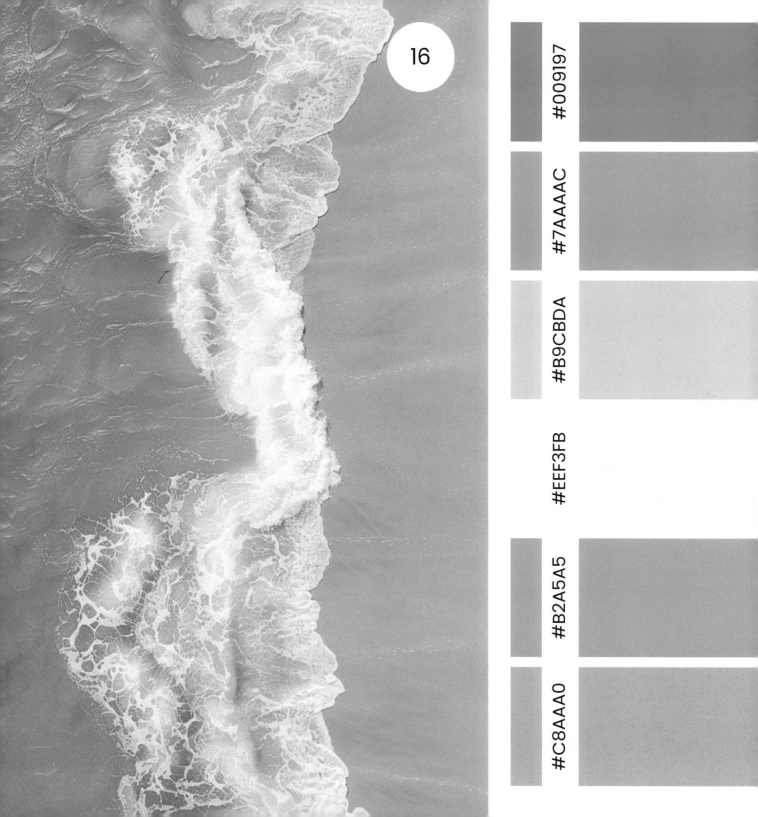

16

#009197

#7AAAAC

#B9CBDA

#EEF3FB

#B2A5A5

#C8AAA0

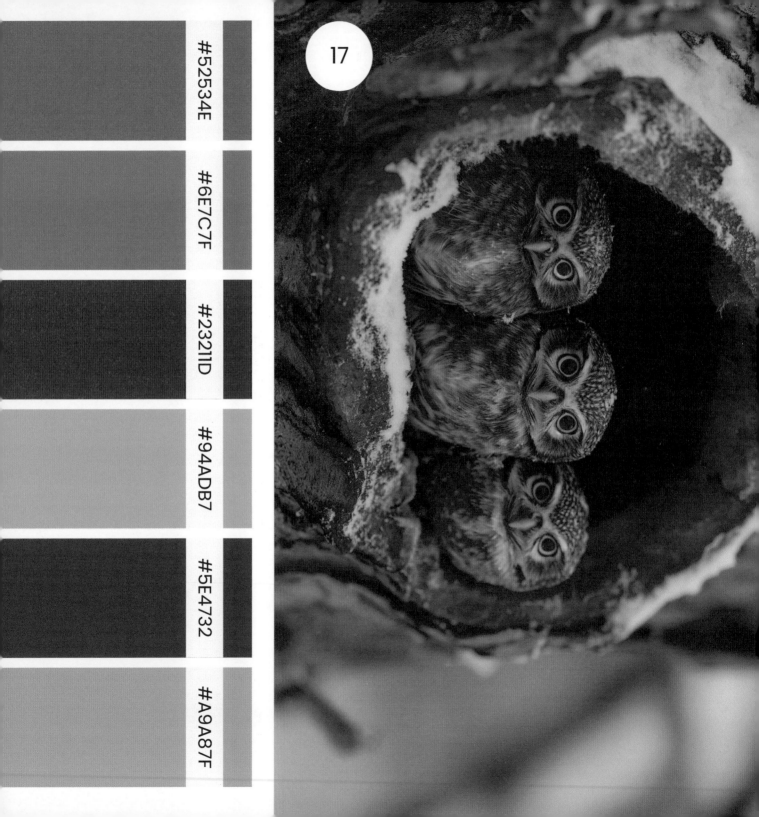

#52534E

#6E7C7F

#23211D

#94ADB7

#5E4732

#A9A87F

18

#ED801F

#51AEBA

#425781

#D2AE5D

#7D5830

#3F2D24

#3D4851

#69747B

#1D2327

#96AFC1

#B19578

#EAA878

20

#B27C5D

#D08D3B

#6D7D74

#836236

#568EA9

#A7C3D9

#3C6AA1

#6692C0

#A0BEDC

#D2E4F0

#1B3F78

#F3FAF9

22

#CCCF71

#B75331

#758336

#5395B4

#A8CAD4

#354422

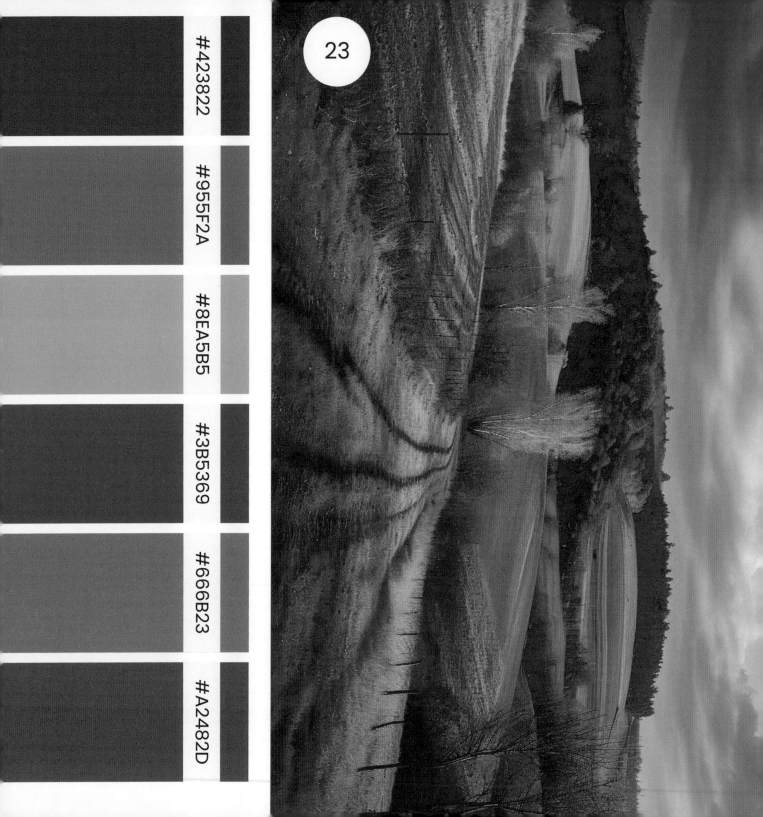

#423822

#955F2A

#8EA5B5

#3B5369

#666B23

#A2482D

23

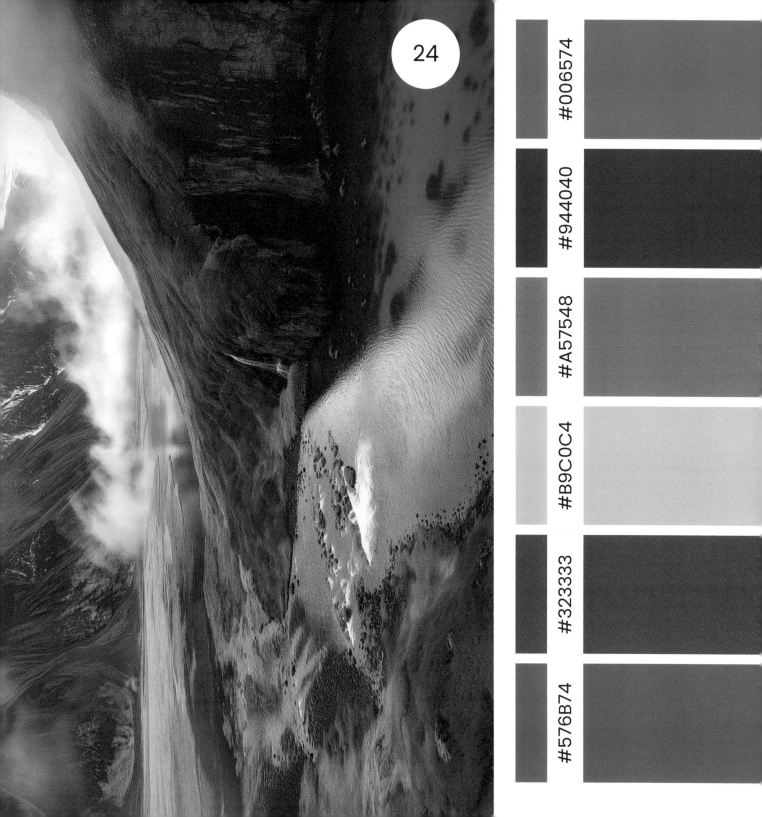

24

#006574

#944040

#A57548

#B9C0C4

#323333

#576B74

#17A7C0

#BD5F1F

#0057BD

#E8AF48

#B2687C

#413546

25

#D3BCBD

#65614E

#8173BB

#3375A6

#7BAED5

#C0CAE6

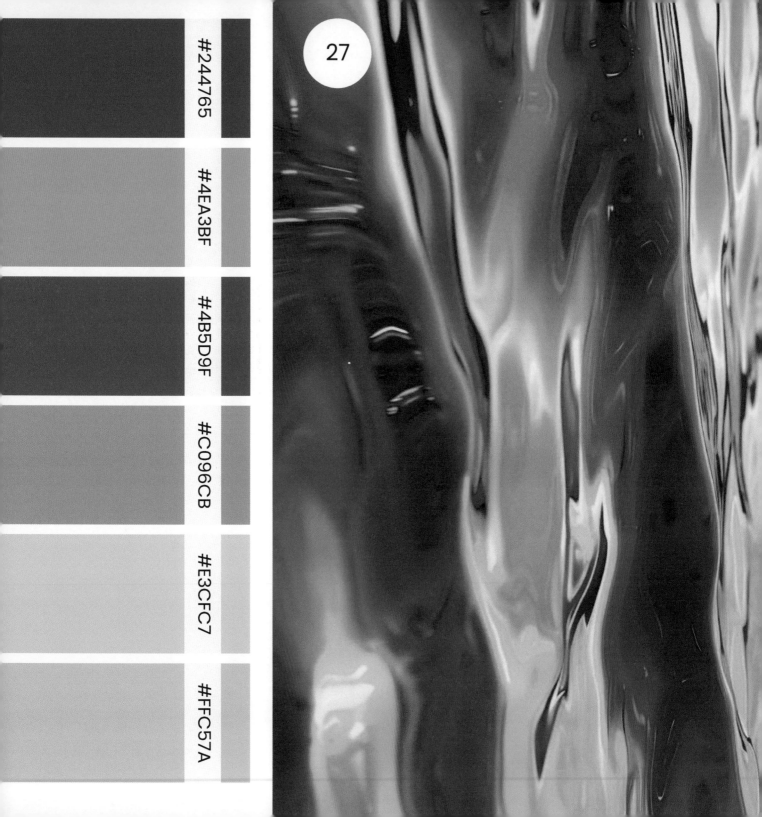

#244765

#4EA3BF

#4B5D9F

#C096CB

#E3CFC7

#FFC57A

27

28

#782F6D

#182A5B

#C96224

#5A395F

#641F2E

#F7B07C

#41425A

#6C4B8B

#7B56C7

#D07DA2

#FFA08B

#F3D0D5

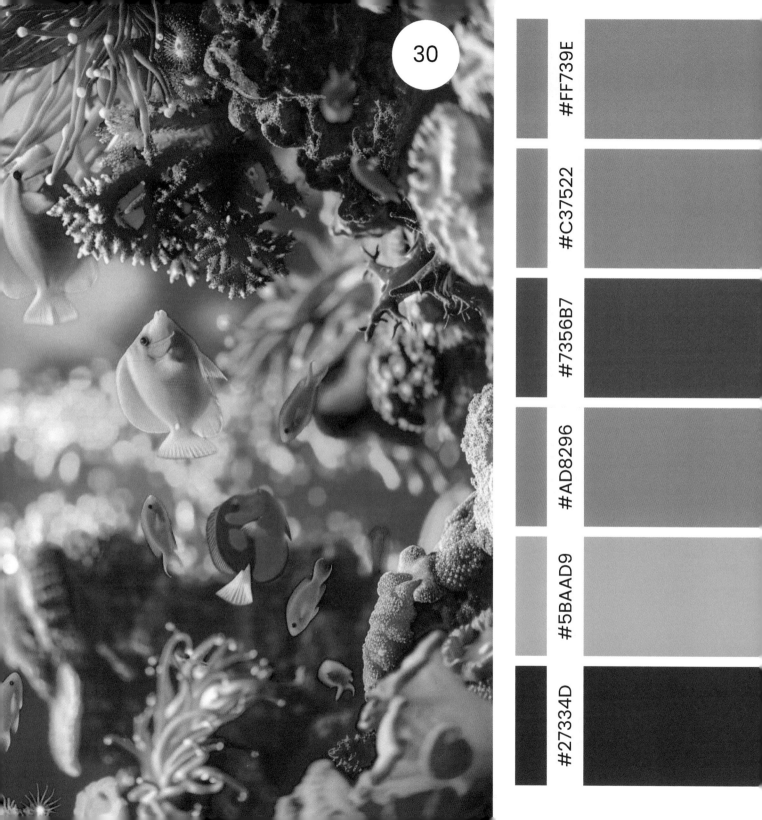

30

#FF739E

#C37522

#7356B7

#AD8296

#5BAAD9

#27334D

#9C9FB5

#526A7D

#90896D

#9D6C69

#776B2C

#E58990

31

32

#FFD1AB

#5A7478

#E6B7B2

#A8A2A6

#689CA4

#886152

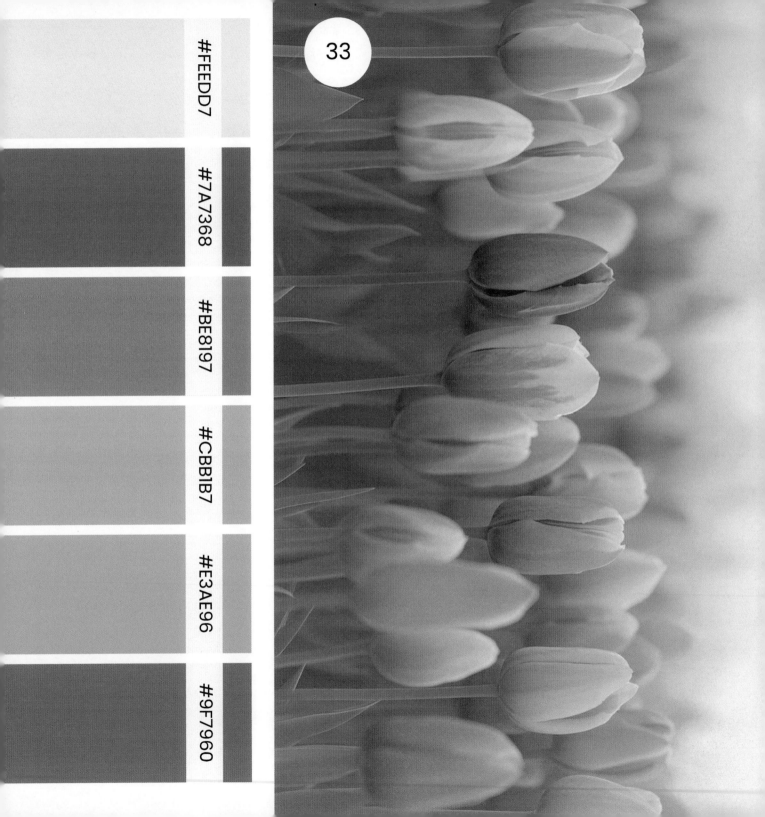

#FEEDD7

#7A7368

#BE8197

#CBB1B7

#E3AE96

#9F7960

33

34

#FFDF8A

#C17961

#814C52

#4F384D

#B48DAA

#7E6C92

#F0E3E9

#927785

#4C5260

#CFABB5

#A5AFB9

#3B5B6C

35

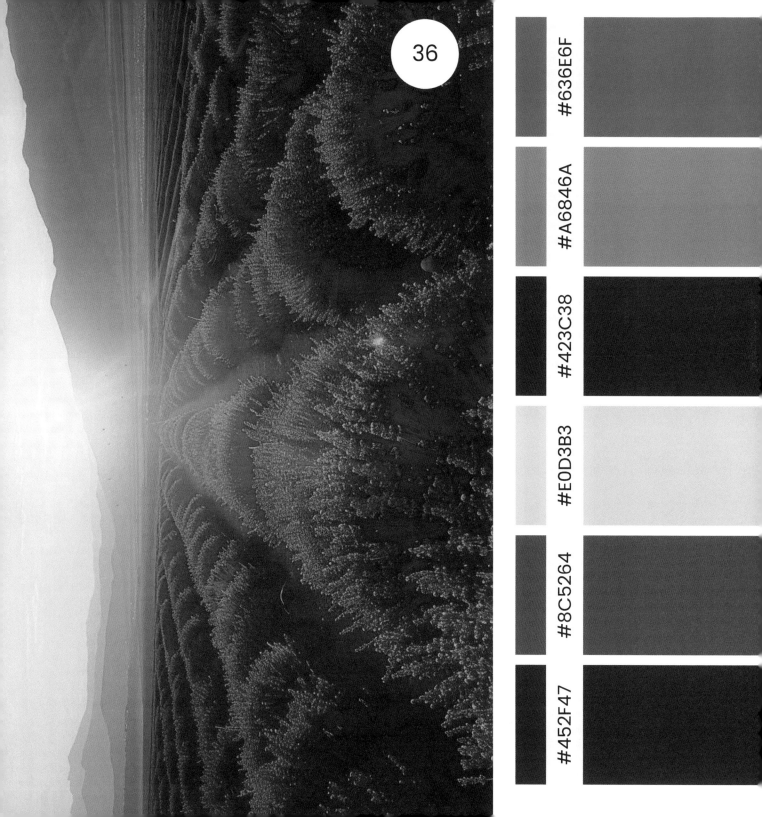

#636E6F

#A6846A

#423C38

#E0D3B3

#8C5264

#452F47

#666195

#F2C9BF

#AA9BC1

#272649

#C17F8C

#F6B595

37

38

#3A222E

#53475F

#C56167

#F8F8F8

#F8F8F8

#F3B4B3

#C2ACBA

#7A788A

#1F2124

#603234

#FF93B2

#EB9A3E

39

40

#F6BF82

#A84F1B

#796955

#CC7D83

#B48981

#9F7E6F

#F6C984

#A64A68

#F5954D

#614D5D

#606A78

#C6A86F

42

#D66F6C

#D3A022

#8DB9E6

#4B5E7A

#494C22

#82844F

#88ABCD

#7E8C2A

#51571E

#B58368A

#D69822

#FC6255

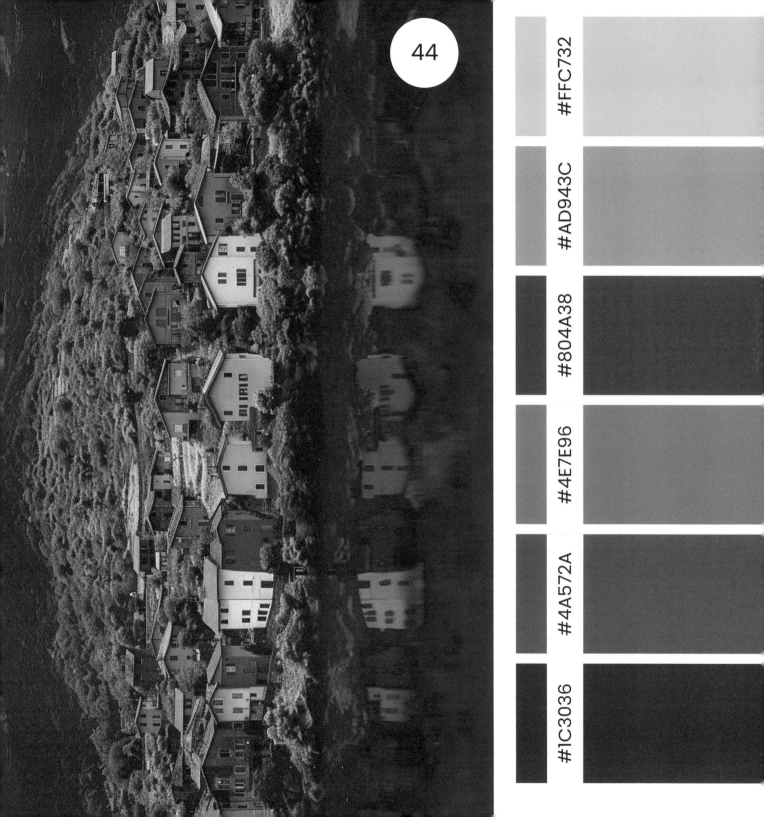

44

#FFC732

#AD943C

#804A38

#4E7E96

#4A572A

#1C3036

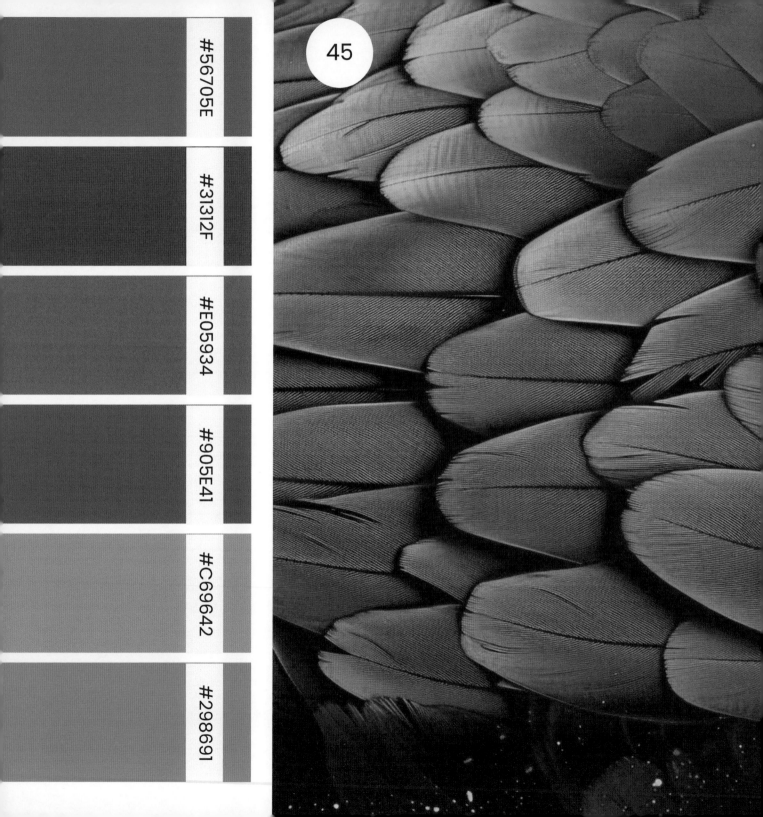

#56705E

#31312F

#E05934

#905E41

#C69642

#298691

#766319

#9D7C45

#8A8884

#E1C18F

#574D32

#27322F

#768597

#203035

#5E6041

#5C260C

#AC6A3C

#F5D4A9

48

#CEB48F

#DA8943

#B04417

#957266

#412421

#733024

#9D2142

#E2722E

#3A4C3F

#0D1C1A

#E0362F

#859477

49

50

#6E785D

#3F4A47

#A89171

#BD5B23

#EDA22D

#C0383E

51

#2B121A

#812632

#52435A

#A27983

#C47E39

#7C7F79

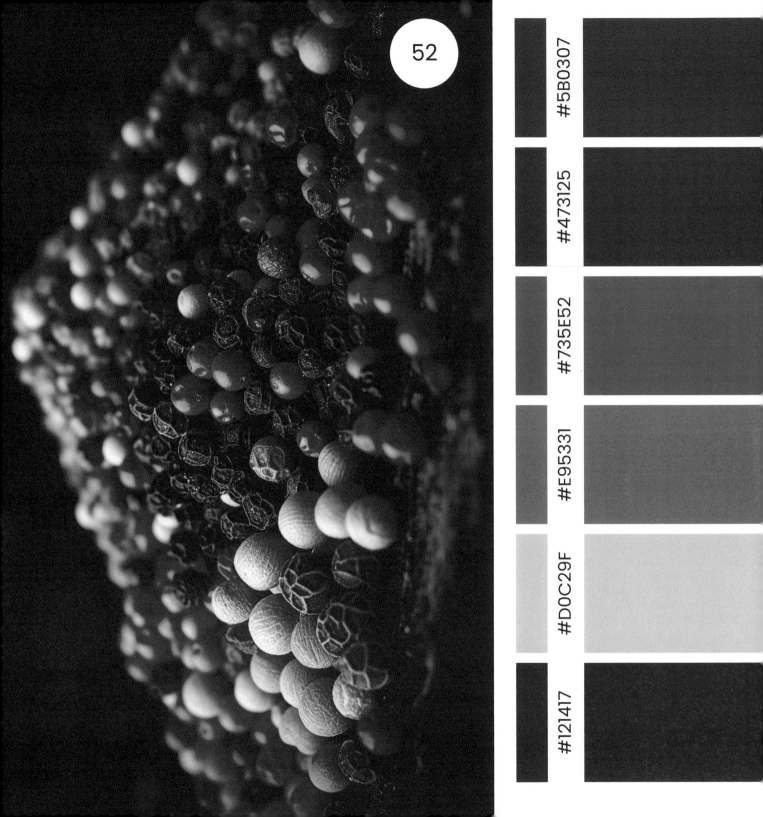

52

#5B0307

#473125

#735E52

#E95331

#D0C29F

#121417

#322822

#5D5A57

#63341E

#D6BA91

#B96A2C

#9F8D6F

54

#73553F

#D4B884

#4A3F37

#DEAC43

#959595

#E1E1E3

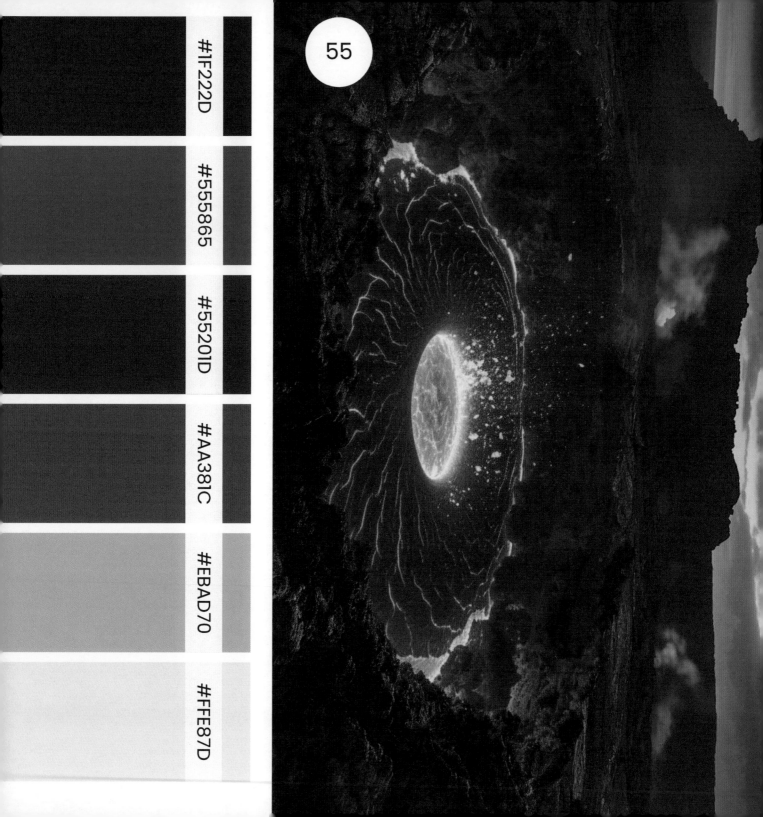

#1F222D

#555865

#55201D

#AA381C

#EBAD70

#FFE87D

56

#FFDF67

#76756E

#CAB490

#D29238

#383514

#78601C

#7F5417

#4C340D

#221A06

#B7923E

#F9EDA6

#D48929

57

58

#896F2D

#52535A

#D49430

#C2945E

#7FA5BA

#CC9071

59

#874734

#8D8F98

#BC692C

#4A3E41

#DCB99F

#FCF5DB

60

#3384C2

#734833

#ECB642

#D5C0A8

#D27724

#96BCE4

#A5B9B2

#CB8631

#E7AA4B

#AA5F17

#A18458

#5E7A79

61

62

#69514B

#774B3E

#8F543C

#372D2A

#72757A

#CD997A

#D5DDE1

#B4AEA5

#71756C

#3B352C

#997251

#994519

64

#262619

#605944

#D2DBDA

#A49E8B

#A7AEA9

#7C8178

Color	Name / Hex	Numbers
	AMBER GOLD #DBB037	8, 18, 42, 54
	IVORY SAND #E0D3B3	36, 52
	BUTTERCREAM #FFDF8A	34, 55, 57
	TANGERINE #FBB72F	1, 25, 44, 60
	STONE TAUPE #7A7368	33
	DESERT SAND #E1C18F	46, 47, 48, 53, 54, 56
	COPPER SPICE #BB8242	10, 11, 20, 24, 41, 43, 45, 51, 56, 57
	GOLDEN HONEY #E7AA4B	45, 58, 61
	PEACH SORBET #FFC57A	27, 38, 41
	HONEY ORANGE #EB9A3E	39, 48, 50, 57, 61
	TOASTED ALMOND #B19578	63
	SUNSET ORANGE #F6821E	2, 18, 41, 49
	RUSTIC AMBER #E8653F	10, 18, 20, 32, 36, 45, 46, 54, 57, 63
	WARM SAND #DCB99F	59, 60
	DESERT PEACH #F7B07C	19, 28, 32, 37, 40, 55
	BURNT SIENNA #BD5F1F	25, 28, 30, 40, 48, 50, 53, 59, 60, 61
	CINNAMON BARK #915A35	4, 20, 33, 45, 47
	SANDY CORAL #CC9071	58, 62

Color	Name / Hex	Numbers
	ANTIQUE TERRA #9F7E6F	40, 48, 54
	DESERT CLAY #C17961	20, 34, 62
	RUSTIC CHESTNUT #804A38	44, 48, 53, 59, 62
	BLUSH BEIGE #C8AAA0	16, 26, 27
	WARM STONE #CCC4C2	13
	FIERY SCARLET #AA381C	55
	CORAL BLUSH #FFA08B	29, 33
	MUTED CORAL #B48981	40
	FLAME RED #F64227	6, 43, 49
	PETAL BLUSH #E6B7B2	32, 37, 38
	CORAL ROSE #D66F6C	42
	MAHOGANY RED #944040	24, 28, 39, 47, 51, 52
	PALE MOCHA #B2A5A5	16
	RUBY RED #C0383E	50
	VINTAGE MAUVE #A07D7F	31, 34, 43, 51
	ROSE QUARTZ #E58990	31, 37, 38, 40
	BALLET PINK #F3D0D5	29
	CRIMSON ROSE #D04B67	9, 41, 49

Color	Name / Hex	Numbers
	ROSE DUST #CBB1B7	33, 35
	STRAWBERRY PINK #FF739E	30, 39
	CRIMSON PLUM #8C5264	36, 41
	DUSKY ROSE #CE8EA8	2, 25, 29, 33
	SOFT PETAL #F0E3E9	35
	VINTAGE PLUM #927785	35, 41
	BERRY ROSE #B36593	7, 29, 38
	SMOKY LILAC #A8A2A6	32
	DUSKY ROSE #B48DAA	34, 39
	SMOKY PLUM #614D5D	41
	PLUM NOIR #452F47	36
	LILAC MINT #C096CB	27
	LAVENDER MIST #EAC7F5	6
	DUSTY VIOLET #7E6C92	34
	LILAC MIST #AA9BC1	37
	SMOKY LILAC #7A788A	39
	SLATE LAVENDER #666195	26, 30, 37
	MIDNIGHT INDIGO #272649	37

Color	Name / Hex	Numbers
	GRAPHITE BLUE #41425A	29, 30, 35, 37
	DARK SLATE BLUE #425781	18, 27, 30
	NAVY BLUE #1B3F78	21, 28
	ROYAL BLUE #0057BD	25
	STEEL BLUE #3C6AA1	21
	STORMY BLUE #3B5369	23, 27, 31, 41, 42
	PALE PERIWINKLE #88ABCD	43, 60
	AZURE BLUE #3384C2	60
	LIGHT STEEL BLUE #A7C3D9	10, 19, 20, 21
	SKY BLUE #8DC0E3	5, 21, 22, 26, 42, 43, 60
	PEWTER BLUE #96AFC1	6, 10, 16, 17, 19, 23, 58
	STORM GRAY #69747B	19, 24, 31, 41, 47, 55, 58, 59, 62
	SILVER MIST #B9C0C4	24, 35, 63
	CORNFLOWER #5AA1D0	7, 20, 21, 22, 26, 30, 60
	POWDER BLUE #D2E4F0	16, 21
	OCEAN BLUE #568EA9	10, 20, 22, 26, 32, 44, 58
	CHARCOAL BLUE #1D2F36	5, 6, 8, 13, 15

Color	Name / Hex	Numbers
	TEAL SLATE #325866	9, 13, 14, 15, 35
	ICE BLUE #A8CAD4	6, 22
	DUSTY OCEAN #4C7E89	14, 15, 24
	PALE SLATE #789AA5	6
	FADED DENIM #5B7379	8, 32, 61
	TROPICAL TEAL #469BAC	11, 18, 27, 45
	TROPICAL AQUA #7FCED5	11, 15
	SERENE AQUA #73A6A7	12, 16, 32
	JADE TEAL #3F9495	13, 14, 16
	SLATE GREEN #4B6F6B	3, 7, 12, 45
	SEAFOAM GREEN #6CAFA4	7, 8, 9, 13
	PALE MINT #C5DBD6	11, 12, 13, 15
	FOREST SLATE #3F4A47	49, 50
	MISTY SAGE #A5B9B2	61
	SAGE FOREST #4B6250	2
	FOREST LEAF #50883D	6
	FOREST GREEN #315020	2, 22

Color	Name / Hex	Numbers
	PALE SAGE #B2C3A1	3
	SAGE MIST #A6AF94	2, 49
	OLIVE DRAB #5A6624	3, 23, 44, 50
	OLIVE GROVE #758336	22, 42
	LIME OLIVE #839427	5, 43
	OLIVE GREEN #A6B261	3, 9
	DEEP FOREST #494C22	42, 43, 47
	LIME ZEST #B8BA37	3
	SAGE KHAKI #A9A87F	17
	MUSTARD OLIVE #857D21	4, 5, 7, 31
	GOLDEN OLIVE #B6AD3D	1
	OLIVE BROWN #645D3D	8, 15
	HARVEST GOLD #C2A92A	4
	GOLDENROD #F4D237	7, 56
	VANILLA CREAM #F2EACB	15, 33, 59
	TAUPE STONE #A49E8B	64
	BRONZE GOLD #AE8E3D	8, 44, 57

Printed in Great Britain
by Amazon

58011848R00041